Level Up! The Guide

How to turn your ideas into your business

The Workbook

B. Marie Blaine

Level Up! The Guide Workbook
How to turn your ideas into your business.

Level Up! The Guide Workbook
How to turn your ideas into your business.

Introduction - Preplanning

What is stopping you from starting your business? List every single issue

Level Up! The Guide Workbook
How to turn your ideas into your business.

CHAPTER 1 - *Who is a part of this company?*

1-1   Whose professional services can enhance your business?

1-2   Who are the partners? (list below)

1-3   Contributions of each Partner

      A.   Initial

      B.   Ongoing

1-3   Terms for admitting New Partners

1-4   How will Profit and Loss be distributed?

1-5   What is management's power and duties?

Chapter 1 Notes

CHAPTER 2 - Mission, Vision and Values

2-1   What is the purpose of your business?

2-2   What do you hope to achieve by running this business?

2-3   Why are you starting this company?

2-4   Write your purpose

2-5   Write the summary of your purpose

Level Up! The Guide Workbook
How to turn your ideas into your business.

2-6   What is your company's mission?

2-7   What is your company's vision?

2-8   What company are you committed to supporting?

2-9   What is their mission and vision?

Chapter 2 Notes

Level Up! The Guide Workbook
How to turn your ideas into your business.

Chapter 3 - Location

3-1   Will your business location be physical or online?

3-2   List your requirements for your location physical or online.

3-3 How are you going to drive traffic into your business?

Level Up! The Guide Workbook
How to turn your ideas into your business.

Chapter 3 Notes

CHAPTER 4 - *What market are you going to target?*

4-1   What does this business do?

4-2   How will the business run?

4-3   Who will buy the product?

4-4   What is your company's main product(s)?

4-5   What else can be added on to the sale?

4-6   What can personalize your product or teach the

consumer how to take care of it?

4-7   Who will have the highest interest?

4-8   Who will buy it for those interested?

4-9   Who is your target market? i.e. Girls 13-19,

Women 50 +

4-10 What individual characteristics will your market

have?

Chapter 4 Notes

Chapter 5 - Finance

5-1 What is needed to start your business? List below each and every item and its cost. Also in the third column list the free option.

Item	Cost	Free Option

Level Up! The Guide Workbook
How to turn your ideas into your business.

5-2 List out what you can do now to start your business.

List all the things that are free or under $100.

5-3   Which professional organizations are you a member?

5-4   Which ones do you want to join?

5-5   What is the cost to join? Go to their website and check it out!

Level Up! The Guide Workbook
How to turn your ideas into your business.

Chapter 5 notes

Level Up! The Guide Workbook
How to turn your ideas into your business.

CHAPTER 6- Incorporation

6-1   Name of business?

6-2   Purpose of business?

6-3   Industry of business?

6-4   How many owners?

6-5   Who are the owners?

6-6   How will the business allocate the profit?

6-7   How will your business create revenue?

Chapter 6 Notes

Chapter 7 - Wrap Up

7-1 What can you do today to start your business?

Additional Notes

Additional Notes

Additional Notes

Additional Notes

www.ingramcontent.com/pod-product-compliance
Lightning Source LLC
Chambersburg PA
CBHW071222240526
45470CB00018B/2289